How does it move?

Bobbie Kalman

🌱 **Crabtree Publishing Company**

www.crabtreebooks.com

Created by Bobbie Kalman

Dedicated by Kathy Middleton
For my wonderful Ava Xian who moves me beyond words.

Author and Editor-in-Chief
Bobbie Kalman

Editor
Kathy Middleton

Proofreader
Crystal Sikkens

Photo research
Bobbie Kalman
Crystal Sikkens

Design
Bobbie Kalman
Katherine Berti
Samantha Crabtree
      (logo and front cover)

Production coordinator
Katherine Berti

Illustrations
Barbara Bedell: pages 9, 11, 15, 18, 19 (fish),
      24 (flying squirrel and monkeys)
Katherine Berti: kangaroos on pages 17, 24
Bonna Rouse: pages 14, 17 (frog), 21, 24 (bird and frog)
Tiffany Wybouw: page 16, dolphins on pages 19, 24

Photographs
© Dreamstime.com: page 13 (right)
© iStockphoto.com: pages 5 (insets), 17 (grasshopper)
© Shutterstock.com: cover, pages 1, 3, 4, 5 (except insets),
      6, 7, 8, 9, 10, 11 (bottom), 12 (except inset), 13 (left), 14,
      15, 16, 17 (children), 18, 19, 21, 22, 23, 24 (except rabbit)
© Albert Kok/Wikipedia: page 20
Other images by Corbis, Corel, and Digital Vision

Library and Archives Canada Cataloguing in Publication

Kalman, Bobbie, 1947-
      How does it move? / Bobbie Kalman.

(Looking at nature)
Includes index.
ISBN 978-0-7787-3322-5 (bound).--ISBN 978-0-7787-3342-3 (pbk.)

      1. Animal locomotion--Juvenile literature. 2. Plants--Irritability and
movements--Juvenile literature. I. Title. II. Series: Kalman, Bobbie,
1947- . Looking at nature.

QP301.K34 2008   j573.7'9   C2008-907023-2

Library of Congress Cataloging-in-Publication Data

Kalman, Bobbie.
   How does it move? / Bobbie Kalman.
      p. cm. -- (Looking at nature)
      Includes index.
      ISBN 978-0-7787-3342-3 (pbk. : alk. paper) -- ISBN 978-0-7787-3322-5
(reinforced library binding : alk. paper)

   1. Animal locomotion--Juvenile literature. 2. Plants--Irritability and
movements--Juvenile literature. I. Title. II. Series.

QP301.K29 2008
573.7'9--dc22

                                          2008046269

Crabtree Publishing Company

www.crabtreebooks.com   1-800-387-7650

Published in Canada
Crabtree Publishing
616 Welland Ave.
St. Catharines, Ontario
L2M 5V6

Published in the United States
Crabtree Publishing
PMB16A
350 Fifth Ave., Suite 3308
New York, NY 10118

Published in the United Kingdom
Crabtree Publishing
White Cross Mills
High Town, Lancaster
LA1 4XS

Published in Australia
Crabtree Publishing
386 Mt. Alexander Rd.
Ascot Vale (Melbourne)
VIC 3032

Contents

How does it move?

Plants, animals, and people are **living things**. Living things change and move. Plants do not move from place to place, but their parts move to reach sunlight or water. People and most animals are able to move from place to place. They move in different ways.

Sunflowers turn their heads to face the sun from morning until evening. They turn very slowly, so it is hard to see them move.

The leaves of mimosa plants **droop**, or hang down, when something touches them. The leaves on this plant drooped when the mouse touched them.

mimosa
plant

Venus flytraps are plants that eat small animals. The leaves of the flytrap snap shut quickly when something touches its hairs. This fly is trapped. The plant will eat it!

Venus
flytrap

Using their legs

Many animals that live on land have legs. They use their legs to move from place to place. Some animals move on four legs. Some animals have even more legs. Animals with legs can walk. Some can run, swing, and climb, too.

*This pony is using its four legs to run on a beach. It is **galloping**, or running very fast. Its **hoofs** are flying above the sand! They do not touch the ground.*

Hoofs are hard feet.

This boy is running on two legs. He puts one leg in front of the other as he runs. He is running very fast, like the pony. His feet lift above the sand as he runs. He can walk on his hands, too, but not very far!

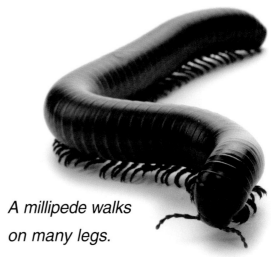

A millipede walks on many legs.

No legs or arms

Some animals do not have legs or arms. These animals slide from place to place. Worms, snakes, snails, and slugs slide along the ground. They slide along rocks and plants.

curve
curve
curve

*Snakes **slither**. To slither is to move in **curves**. Curves are lines that are bent. Snakes make curves in their bodies. They then use the curved parts to push themselves forward. This snake is using three big curves to move forward.*

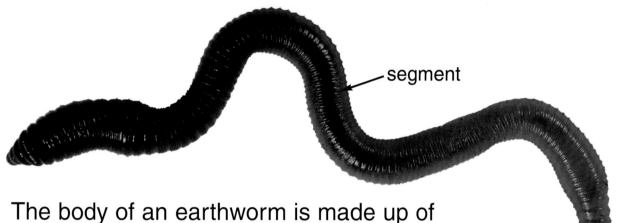

segment

The body of an earthworm is made up of many **segments**. Segments are parts. To move, a worm stretches out some of its segments. The other segments then pull forward.

snail

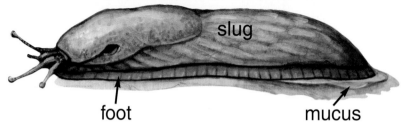

slug

foot

mucus

Snails are animals with shells. Slugs are like snails without shells.

*Each snail and slug moves on one **foot** on the bottom of its body. Snails and slugs make **mucus** in their bodies. Mucus is like slime. The mucus coats the ground under the animals. The foot then slides on the mucus.*

Climb and swing

Some animals live high up in trees. Some animals climb trees to look for food. Others climb when they are in danger. Animals have different body parts that help them climb.

Tree frogs live in trees. Their sticky toes help them climb.

tree bark

claws

*This black bear is using its claws to climb a tree. **Claws** grip tree **bark**. They keep the bear from slipping.*

sticky toes

The arms of monkeys and apes are longer than their legs are. Long arms help these animals swing from tree to tree.

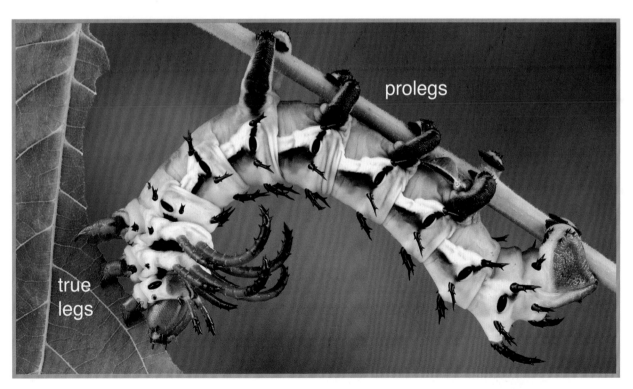

prolegs

true
legs

*A caterpillar uses its six **true legs** like hands to hold the leaf it is eating. Its ten **prolegs** are not real legs, but they help a caterpillar climb, crawl, and hang.*

11

Up the mountain

Some animals live high on mountains. Climbing rocks on mountains can be slippery! Many mountain animals have hoofs with two toes for climbing. Hoofs with two toes grip rocks and do not slip off.

hoofs with two toes

mountain goats

People do not have hoofs, but they still love to climb mountains. Some practice on rock climbing walls first. Some people ski down mountains, instead of climbing them. Whether you climb or ski, you should always wear a helmet!

Don't look down!

13

flapping

gliding

Flying high!

Birds, bats, and some insects have wings. They can fly. Birds **flap** to lift off the ground. To flap is to move wings up and down. When birds are high in the sky, they can **glide**. When they glide, the air carries them along. They do not have to flap their wings.

Bats can fly, but they cannot glide. They must keep flapping their wings to move through the air.

The wings of bats have thin skin. You can see their arm bones!

Butterflies have four wings for flying. They can also glide.

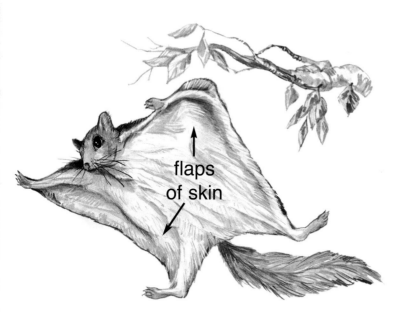

flaps of skin

*Flying squirrels do not really fly. They glide as they jump from tree to tree. They have **flaps** of skin between their legs that they use for gliding.*

*Hummingbirds **hover**. To hover is to stay in one place in the air. Hummingbirds flap their wings quickly to stay in place.*

15

Hop and leap

frog

kangaroo

Some animals take big jumps to get from here to there. Kangaroos, frogs, grasshoppers, and rabbits jump. Animals that jump have strong back legs. Their back legs are longer than their front legs are.

grasshopper

frog

rabbit

We use different words to describe how animals jump.

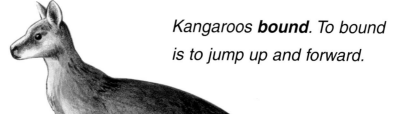

Kangaroos **bound**. To bound is to jump up and forward.

Bunnies **hop**. To hop is to take small jumps.

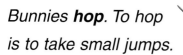

Grasshoppers do not hop. They can leap both very high and very far!

Frogs **leap**. To leap is to take a big, quick jump.

Which of these children are leaping, hopping, or bounding?

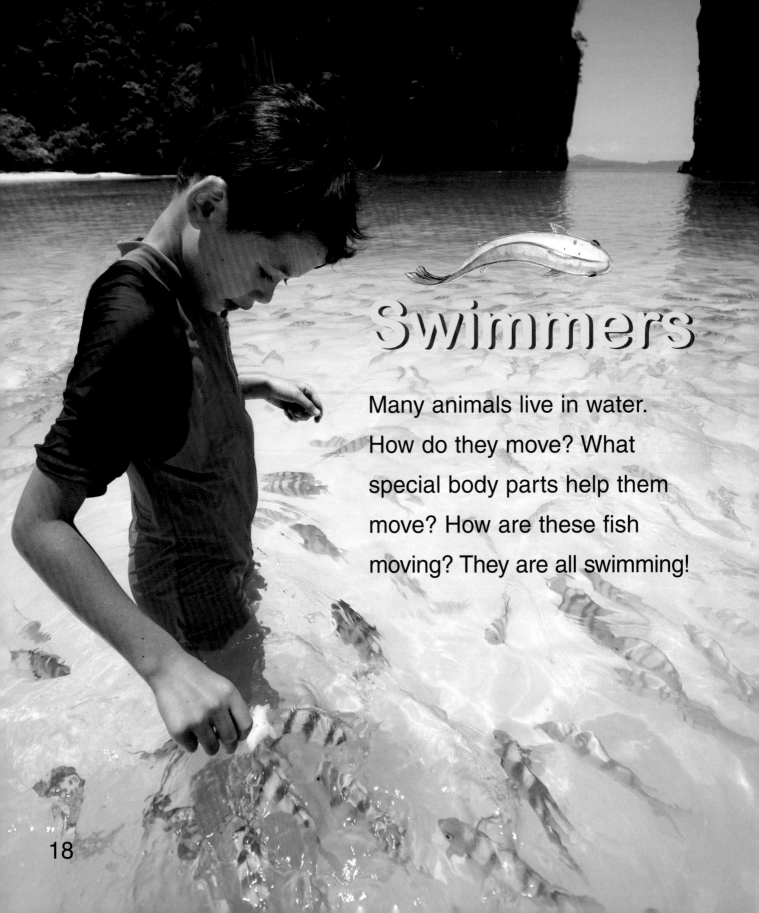

Swimmers

Many animals live in water. How do they move? What special body parts help them move? How are these fish moving? They are all swimming!

Fish swim by moving their bodies from side to side. They swish their tail **fins** back and forth.

fin

Dolphins live in water, but they are not fish. To swim, they move their **flippers**, or tails, up and down.

flipper

*Dolphins **porpoise** while they travel.*
To porpoise is to move quickly by leaping out of water.

Moving in water

Some water animals do not swim the way dolphins or fish do. Their bodies move in other ways. How do these animals move?

Octopuses take water into their bodies and then shoot it out. The jet of water pushes them forward. Their arms trail behind them.

swan

duck

webbed feet

Ducks, geese, and swans live on water. They have **webbed** feet. Webbed feet have skin between the toes. Water birds use their webbed feet like paddles.

goose

Penguins are birds that swim under water. They use their short wings to fly through water.

penguin

How do you move?

People can move in different ways. We can move the way many animals move. These children are moving like some animals you know. Which animal makes and climbs a web that looks like this?

web

spider

dolphin

Which animal leaps high out of water?

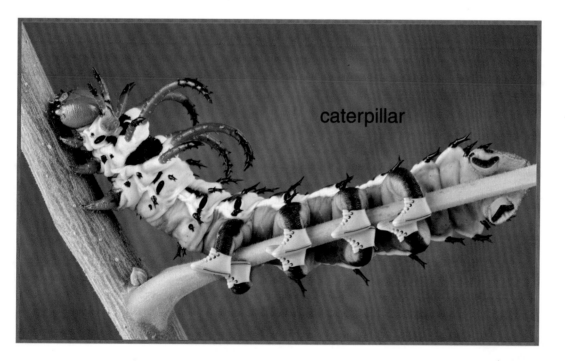

caterpillar

How many shoes is this caterpillar wearing to run a race with you? How many shoes are four times two?

Words to know and Index

bounding
page 17

climbing
pages 6, 10,
11, 12, 13, 22

flying
pages 14,
15, 21

gliding
pages 14, 15

Other index words

arms pages 8, 11, 15, 20
claws page 10
crawling page 11

hopping
pages
16, 17

leaping
pages 16,
17, 19, 23

running
pages 6,
7, 23

feet pages 9, 21
flapping pages 14, 15
hoofs pages 6, 12, 13
jumping pages 15, 16–17
legs pages 6–7, 8, 11,
15, 16
people pages 4, 7, 13,
17, 22
plants pages 4–5, 8
toes pages 10, 12, 21
walking pages 6, 7
wings pages 14–15, 21

slithering
page 8

swimming
pages 18,
19, 20, 21

swinging
pages 6,
10, 11

24

Printed in the U.S.A. - BG